OPEN EYE, OPEN HEART

Selected Works by Lawrence Ferlinghetti

POETRY

Pictures of the Gone World (City Lights Books, 1955)
A Coney Island of the Mind (New Directions, 1958)
Translation: Jacques Prévert, *Paroles*
(City Lights Books, 1958)
Starting from San Francisco (New Directions, 1967)
The Secret Meaning of Things (New Directions, 1968)
Back Roads to Far Places (New Directions, 1971)
Open Eye, Open Heart (New Directions, 1973)

PROSE

Her (New Directions, 1960)
Tyrannus Nix? (New Directions, 1969)
The Mexican Night (New Directions, 1970)

PLAYS

Unfair Arguments with Existence (New Directions, 1963)
Routines (New Directions, 1964)

FILMS

Have You Sold Your Dozen Roses? (1960)
Tyrannus Nix? (N.E.T., 1969)
Assassination Raga, with Max Crosley (1973)

RECORDINGS

Poetry Readings in "The Cellar," with Kenneth Rexroth
(Fantasy LP7002, 1958)
*Tentative Description of a Dinner to Impeach
President Eisenhower & Other Poems* (Fantasy LP7004, 1959)
The World's Great Poets, Volume 1, with Allen Ginsberg
and Gregory Corso, Spoleto Festival, 1965
(CMS LP617, 1971)
Tyrannus Nix? & Assassination Raga (Fantasy LP7014, 1971)

LAWRENCE FERLINGHETTI

OPEN EYE,
OPEN HEART

A NEW DIRECTIONS BOOK

ACKNOWLEDGMENTS

Grateful thanks are given to the editors and publishers of the various pub-
lications in which many of the poems in this book first appeared: *Antaeus,
Bastard Angel, The Berkeley Barb, Big Sky, Bulletin from Nothing, Cafe
Solo, The Carolina Quarterly, Chelsea Review, Choice, El Corno Emplu-
mado, East Village Other, Evergreen Review, Isis, Liberation, Mediter-
ranean Review, The Montreal Gazette, New Directions in Prose and Poetry,
The Nation, The New York Times Book Review, The New York Quarterly,
Pomegranate Broadsides, San Francisco Chronicle, San Francisco Phoenix,
Second Coming, The Sunday Paper, Tansy, Transatlantic Review,
The Village Voice.*

Manufactured in the United States of America
First published clothbound (ISBN: 0-8112-0488-x) and as New Directions
Paperbook 361 (ISBN: 0-8112-0489-8) in 1973
Published simultaneously in Canada by McClelland & Stewart, Ltd.

New Directions Books are published for James Laughlin
by New Directions Publishing Corporation,
333 Sixth Avenue, New York 10014

SECOND PRINTING

CONTENTS

I. Open Eye, Open Heart

TRUE CONFESSIONAL   3

MOCK CONFESSIONAL   6

IN A TIME OF REVOLUTION FOR INSTANCE   10

THE ASTONISHED HEART   13

SUEÑO REAL   16

BIG SUR GRASS REVERIE   20

FUGITIVE CONFIGURATIONS   21

THE REAL MAGIC OPERA BEGINS   23

STONE REALITY MEDITATION   26

SUNRISE, BOLINAS   27

SONG OF LOVE & DESIRE   28

PLEASE, ETERNAL WOMAN, DON'T . . .   29

AT KENNETH REXROTH'S   31

A PHOENIX AT FIFTY   32

THE MAN WHO RODE AWAY   34

AN ELEGY ON THE DEATH OF KENNETH PATCHEN   37

POEM FOR OLD WALT   40

II. Poems in Transit

INTO DARKNESS, IN GRANADA   43

A GIACOMETTI SUMMER   44

AN IMAGINARY HAPPENING, LONDON   45

LONDON, RAINY DAY   46

THOUGHTS TO A CONCERTO OF TELEMANN   47

CRO-MAGNONS   49

SEVERAL SURREALIST LITANIES FOR A FILM ON THE
    CEMETERY OF PÈRE LACHAISE   50

TOC TOC: A COUPLE OBSERVED   54

TROIS POÈMES SPONTANÉS SUR LA FORCE DE FRAPPE
    DE L'AMOUR À SIX HEURES DU MATIN   55

POUND AT SPOLETO   58

WOODEN RUSSIA STILL   60

PERPETUAL REVOLUTION   61

POEMS FROM 'RUSSIAN WINTER JOURNAL'   62

MOON SHOT   67

A SPIDER   69

III. Public & Political Poems

CONCRETE POLITICS   73

A PARADE TIRADE   74

TELEGRAM FROM SPAIN   76

WHERE IS VIETNAM?   77

SALUTE   79

THE THIRD WORLD   81

ENIGMA OF HO CHI MINH'S FUNERAL   83

LETTER TO A YOUNG POET IN CUBA OR MAYBE SPAIN   85

A WORLD AWASH WITH FASCISM AND FEAR   87

BASEBALL CANTO   93

LAS VEGAS TILT   96

FORTY ODD QUESTIONS FOR THE GREEK REGIME
      AND ONE CRY FOR FREEDOM   109

CARNAVAL DE MAÏZ   112

ALASKA PIPE DREAM   114

IV. American Mantra & Songs

MOTHER OF LIGHT MANTRA   117

BIG SUR SUN SUTRA   120

LAUGHING & CRYING   121

NIGHT LIGHT   123

TANTRIC BALLAD   125

IDOL CHANT   127

GREAT CHAIN CHANT   128

AIRPORT MANTRA   129

SPONTANEOUS ANARCHIST PACIFIST BUDDHIST SONG   130

NINE SHAMAN SONGS RESUNG   132

STREETS OF SAN FRANCISCO   144

BALLAD OF THE BOAT-KEEPER   146

Open Eye, Open Heart

TRUE CONFESSIONAL

I was conceived in the summer of Nineteen Eighteen
(or was it Thirty Eight)
when some kind of war was going on
but it didn't stop two people
from making love in Ossining that year
I like to think on a riverbank in sun
on a picnic by the Hudson
as in a painting of the Hudson River School
or up at Bear Mountain maybe
after taking the old Hudson River Line
paddlewheel excursion steamer
(I may have added the paddlewheel—
the Hudson my Mississippi)
And on the way back she
already carried me
inside of her
I lawrence ferlinghetti
wrought from the dark in my mother long ago
born in a small back bedroom—
In the next room my brother heard
the first cry,
many years later wrote me—
"Poor Mom—No husband—No money—Pop dead—
How she went through it all—"
Someone squeezed my heart
to make it go
I cried and sprang up
Open eye open heart where
do I wander
I cried and ran off
into the heart of the world
Carried away

by another I knew not
And which of me shall know my brother?
'I am my son, my mother, my father,
I am born of myself
my own flesh sucked'
And someone squeezed my heart
to make me go
And I began to go
through my number
I was a wind-up toy
someone had dropped wound-up
into a world already
running down
The world had been going on
a long time already
but it made no difference
It was new it was like new
i made it new
i saw it shining
and it shone in the sun
and it spun in the sun
and the skein it spun
was pure light
My life was made of it
made of the skeins of light
The cobwebs of Night
were not on it
were not of it
It was too bright
to see
too luminous
to cast a shadow
and there was another world
behind the bright screens
I had only to close my eyes

4

for another world to appear
too near and too dear
to be anything but myself
my inside self
where everything real
was to happen
in this place which still exists
inside myself
and hasn't changed that much
certainly not as much
as the outside
with its bag of skin
and its 'aluminum beard'
and its blue blue eyes
which see as one eye
in the middle of the head
where everything happens
except what happens
in the heart
vajra lotus diamond heart
wherein I read
the poem that never ends

MOCK CONFESSIONAL

Fish-sky at morning
and why should I
tell the world about it
It's not the kind of news
makes headlines down here
Anyway I hear people are wondering about me
and I've written this to clear the air
especially since
people who read my books
don't read other books
I'm sometimes known as the creator
of the immortal line
'When I was a boy I was my father'
I generally feel like kissing someone
when I'm asleep
I don't like sweet wine and cigarettes
police and bitchy women
Otherwise I'm amenable
to what goes down out here
I know I'll never amount to anything
I don't want to amount to
which is not to say I'm without ambition
Sometimes I feel a fluttering in me
and I may sometime fly into the sun
wearing wax wings
I have a feeling I'm falling
on rare occasions
but most of the time I have my feet on the ground
I can't help it if the ground itself is falling
I sometimes wonder what my totem animal is
In any case I'm not a crow or a grey fox
I may be somewhere between a centaur

and Sancho Panza's ass
I know a good thing when I see it
and intend to survive
even if it means being a survivor
I have strange dreams sometimes
but they're not half as weird as
what I see walking down the street
I never did like people who walk like
they're on their way to a party
When I'm at cocktail parties
I usually don't say what I'm thinking
which results in the usual drunkenness
I can't help it if Catholic priests
won't accept my confession
that I consider the Immaculate Conception
a cock-and-bull story
and always viewed the world as a *mons veneris*
After all Father
there must have been plans
for more than two Comings
If this sounds like bright cocktail chatter
remember I'm drinking out of desperation
I believe in the Revolution
in its double-edged image
but baby yours is not mine
I refuse to confess to the boys
or the ladies in the bathroom
What could they be up to
which I am not up to
Why don't we all just dance and sing
and let the appendages hang out where they will
Let's forge on to simpler things
The last time I saw Paris
was in the winter of 1967
when I had to sleep in a windowless room

in a street whose name I'd rather not remember
since I insisted in staying in the same hotel
I'd stayed in as a student a century ago
which now was made over into a mattress factory
Some days I just don't know what to make of things
Other days I'm sure I have the solution to everything
the little key that will fit everything
and turn everything to my own alchemy
if not the wooden key that mayors give you
Well I'll have to begin again
It seems my personal life is a complete fuck-up
though I'm a raving success in the field
While I'm catching the high fly
a worm has succeeded in eating
a hole in my soul
When I reach down to mend it
I find a cocoon in my crotch
which becomes a butterfly as I watch
While I'm zipping up
it flits to my heart
And the world begins again
With a lurch it starts whirling once more
with its little supercargo of flesh
The race horses in their slots
take off again
but the big board registers Tilt
when someone like the government
jiggles the machine
As I was saying it seems
I'm a complete failure on the home-front
and my key won't fit my own door anymore
but that's still no sign I'm not an artistic triumph
I've proved that already with my fearless pen
though now it may run dry
and I have to dip it in some body fluid to continue

of which there are only two symbolic choices:
blood or water
The moving finger writes in both
and fumbles on
but leaves its indelible traces
only in one
which makes me wonder
if I really choose to be immortal
Excuse me for a moment
There's another butterfly
lighted on my fly
and my metamorphosis
may not be done
though now I am 'old'
and am my son

IN A TIME OF REVOLUTION
FOR INSTANCE

I had just ordered a fishplate at the counter when
three very beautiful
fucked-up people entered
I don't know how or why I
thought they must be
fucked-up except
they were very beautiful
two men and one very
beautiful goldenhaired
young woman very
well groomed and
wearing sports clothes like
as if they must have
just gotten out of an
old-fashioned Stutz
roadster with top
down and tennis rackets and
the woman strode to the back
of the restaurant
found a vacant table and
strode back and
got the other two
beckoning with elegant
gestures and
smiling slightly at them and
the three of them
walked back slowly to the table
as if they were not afraid
of anything or anyone
in that place and
took possession of it with

lovely expressions and
the very lovely young lady
settled herself so easily
on the settee beside
the younger of the two men
both of whom had
lightbrown wavy hair not too long
and cut like Hollywood
tennis stars or anyway
like visitors from some other town more
elegant than our own and
they were obviously so much better
looking and so much better
brought up than anyone else
in the place
they looked like they might be
related to the Kennedys and
they obviously had no Indian or Eyetalian
blood in them
and she obviously with
so many avenues open to her
with her two men
one of whom could have been
her brother
I could not imagine her *carrying*
a carbine and
she kept tossing her hair ever so gently out
of her eyes and
smiling at both of them and
at nothing in particular that I
could imagine and
her lips were moving gently with
her gentle smile and
I kept trying to imagine what
she could possibly be saying with

11

those perfect lips over
those perfect teeth so white
with her eyes now and then sliding
over and down the counter where
a lot of little people sat
quietly eating their quite ordinary
lunches while
the three beautiful people who
could have been anywhere
seemed just about to order
something special and
eat it with ice cream and cigarettes and
my fish finally arrived looking
not quite unfrozen and
quite plastic but
I decided to eat it anyway
she was a beautiful creature and I
felt like Charlie Chaplin eating his shoe
when her eyes slid over me
the Modern Jass Quartet
came over the Muzak speakers and
under other circumstances
in a time of revolution for instance
she might have fucked me

THE ASTONISHED HEART

She of the shining eyes
in the next booth
Ramada Inn Lawrence Kansas
Beautiful teeth and long hair
talking to a smiler in sharkskin
She is twenty and aglow
saying something important
about their life together
It must be serious
the way she looks at him
with her far-eyed look
half-smiling
or maybe it is just about the tragedy
of some movie she's just been to
I can't hear the words
Just the voice lisping a little
flat almost
except for the eyes
He smiles into them
They are both smiling
into each other
Maybe it is just a little joke
between them
not a tragedy at all
There is nothing to do about it
in either case
Just watch it happen
amazed and aghast
at the fantastic craziness of it
and of existence
which just goes on
bowling us over

13

Set 'em up in the other alley
Wow watch this one
I got my crystal spectacles on
Soon soon their supper will come
Soon soon they will eat it
or each other
not necessarily a tragedy
She is giving him her
long look again
Soon the curious plastic-antique restaurant
will curl up around them
and blow away with them
over the plains of Kansas
not necessarily
an ecological tragedy
Maybe it is all just a goofy movie
about eating
He may be about to eat a fish
whose baked eye glares up at him
Soon soon they will devour each other
Eyes feasting on each other
each prepares the other's surrender
Soon she will look away
with her long look
out a window
through the Standard Station's neons
toward the plains
where somewhere soon
they will lie together hot
under the sun at noon
Soon soon she will finish eating
her appetizer
Soon soon she will look at him again
You can tell she's still hungry
Woman is a wonderful invention

of man
And man a wonderful invention
of woman
Soon soon they will be born again in the sun
Soon too soon they will be wonderfully done
with each other
She looks away from him now
into the great American night
and seems to see very far
unless it's just contact lenses
making her eyes
so shiny
There is a great crowded bluff
in Lawrence Kansas
that looks a long way
into the astonished heart
of America

SUEÑO REAL

1.

In the eternal dream-time
        a fish dreamt ocean
        a bird sky
And I stand on the beach in the land
    where all is still frontier
And hold an aluminum bird in my hand
And don't dream sand
        running through my head
            as through an hourglass

2.

In the eternal dream-time
  a sigh
      falls from the sky
from some other history than our own
         as if the world were almost
        brand new

3.

Ah, como la tierra es buena
   y la vida—
      la vida es un sueño real . . .
Sun on fire
      sucked into ocean
   And the only shadow
         the shadow of desire afire

4.

      In the eternal dream-time

a whale of a man
          in a great round
                    Mexican sombrero
     with a wide-open
          painted eye on it
suddenly appears
         on the beach by the woods
   The sun
        casts its shadow
              on the ground

5.

Back at the cabin in the woods by the stream
   the white copy of Venus Aphrodite
    stands silent on the porch
  Silk cobwebs on her
     glisten and quiver in wind
       lyre-strands strung
          from head to shoulder
The stream below
          sheds its multi-murmuring
   A million
      spirit-voices
     undertone to birds
         in lush trees above
  A bee browses
       on the alabaster breasts
    and moves
       to the very mouth of Venus
    who is no longer a copy
Ah, aaah
    the universe breathes
A bat
   scrunches up
      under the eaves

6.

Loony surrealist dream
   of a lead soldier in a
             tin cowboy hat
     riding over
          the burnt horizon
        backwards on his horse
In his hand he holds
           a small white horse
       bearing a small white cowboy
              between its teeth
And this cowboy is singing
         'Life is a real dream'

7.

And I went out in the dark dawn
  in the morning of the world
    in the first morning
      and saw the Northern Cross
       with a slow thrust
          bury itself in the mountain
            and burn there in white fire
     huge Excalibur
         stuck in stone

8.

What is that bird
           trying to call my attention?
I've been fifty years
         waiting for this moment
           of light

  And he took it

9.

I know that I don't dream
    'Life
        dreams me'
It is life
      that dreams around me
The leaves breathe
        the hills
            breathe
There is a willow aflame
          with sun
There are a series
       of waterproof mouths
And my words are
      myself. . . .

10.

Transliteration of inanimate objects
    into real beings . . .
        a palimpsest
          an illegible
            manuscreed
        Braille
           night-thought spoke
      by a stream impossible
          to decipher. . . .

BIG SUR GRASS REVERIE

Everything reduced to its essence deduced from its essentials
and I have a choice between laughing & weeping
A bee buzzes in my guitar A burro brays up the canyon of time
A dog adrift unwinds its tail in eternity A tail turned to a
crank turns out barks
And a lovely galloping pony on the wall in my small daughter's
drawing shakes its long mane and becomes my daughter
ready for slaughter A child's play is her first attempt at
living & loving
And a girl walking down the steep high road through the trees
awake becomes a walking fertility root with brown breasts
and legs attached to the earth lush brown goddess darling
take me
And a fat man remains a fat mannikin in a magazine but is also
a ball-bearing baboon ashake with laughter after a fuck
And a tall man walking is a walking phallus in a kingdom of
clitori afire afloat on a stream long hair streaming & the
lips singing Byebye Now I am not mad The end is just be-
ginning and all is tragic with joy

FUGITIVE CONFIGURATIONS

Fugitive configurations
figures on a distant cliff
our bodies soon
all blown away
all transitory all imaginary
graceless
stuttering
Nothing exists
beyond nothing
We are
Nothing
but ephemera scribbled
on a distant landscape
brushed away
light out of light
flickered
I
long to look
in your eyes—
imaginary one
transitory being

Crickets wake me
out of that deep
I rise and look
over the sea
in first morning
It
is a great grey eye
pearl pupil
glimmering
opening & closing
its lace
eyelashes

We constantly
        wake to a dream
        deeper than sleep
Figures
        on a cliff erased
  Lips upon the beach
                        washed out
        Sea's mouth
                yawning utters
                Ocean's long withdrawing OM
They
        are swimming through it
  They
        are surfing in it
                        through the lashes
    They
        are drowning in it
                        Panic ephemera
        ah ah the
                skillful yachts
                        still pass over
Eye winks
        open
            Oh
                I
                am open
                        I look
                into the grey deeps

                        dark dark

        I look
                into your eyes
                        imaginary woman

22

THE REAL MAGIC OPERA BEGINS

In our tatami room
                        our Sacred Jar of Life
            stands full of silence
                                full of light
                in the still white air
And all our 'gods'
                        are silent
                                They
                have nothing more to say
                        to any of us
                        assembled here

What else what else
                        to be aware of
                with our 'expanded consciousness'
                and our 'total awareness'

And how much more Reality
                                is there to be aware of
                is there for us to grin and bear?

My autoharp
                has no answer
            nor any further need to sing

Daniel Moore's Tibetan horn
                                stands echoing
                        and no longer wails
                            ragas of ecstasy
                            ragas of despair
                    in the still white air

And a lovely Japanese platter
    presented to me by the father
    of a young dead Sansei friend
        stands upright on its stand in light
            silent as he is silenced
                        in the silent air
                        of night

Incense stand stands smokeless
Bronze vajra lies all still
            floating lotus petals shut
                        on pure Nothingness
            above which
                        dead brilliant butterflies
                hang pinned up very high
        with nowhere else to fly
                nowhere else to die

Silent Shiva dances still
    inside a silent wheel
            with extra arms akimbo

And a hanging seed scroll symbol
    still receives its flying seed of light
        in the wind which speaks of life
        where we have thought to be
                        very high

As the light falls on earth
    on us assembled here
As the light falls like silence itself
                        which is light
        And the freaked-out wind
                stops howling
                through the high passes

And the still rain starts falling—
   the soft still rain
     the soft voice of rain
       sweet voice of rain
           on summer grasses
      on a lighted mesa
         very high up
           very far away

And the lotus floats free
         in the rain of pure light

And the real magic opera begins

STONE REALITY MEDITATION

Humankind can indeed bear
very much reality
That 'busy little monster
                              manunkind'
can bear it too
So may womankind
So can every kind
of clay and creature
Trees too can bear it
after the leaves have flown away
after the birds have blown away
'bare ruined choirs' bear it
as stones do
They too bear the 'heavy weight
of creation'
as we do
cast in clay and stoned in earth
Masters of ecstasy

SUNRISE, BOLINAS

This little heart that remembers
                    every little thing
          begins the day
                    most of the time
                              by an attempt at singing
                              some sunny rhyme

Such effrontery, such audacity
                    in the face of everything!
Still I'll sing at the sun
                    for a beginning—

Such presumption, such perversity
                    to mistake bird-cries for song
                              when they may really be
                              cries of despair!
          As if our life
               as if all life
                    were not a tragedy
                         though all is passing fair

          As if our life
                    were not so very various
                         as to turn it all to litany—

O drunk flute
               O Golden Mouth
                         sing a mad song
                              to save us

SONG OF LOVE & DESIRE

(After E. A. Poe)

Love is the strangest bird
that ever winged about the world
and whirled and flashed at us
                    its dark marked wings
And stranger still
the image of the loved one
that gestures through our sleep
and drifts from us
through every crowd and cloud
and shift of season
O dark of hair
In sleep we see her body singing half aloud
its alabaster song
We see the parted lips
We hear the muteless voice
struck through the so-called "sad études
of human reason"
Dark of hair O dark of hair
désir délire
desire lost and dreaming
Thy so-called classic face
Thy so-called naiad airs
do make me roam

PLEASE, ETERNAL WOMAN, DON'T...

Now that we have examined your lips
O Eternal Woman
and decided why the curve
of the lower lip smiling
or mouth half-open
should dispel the world
at a glance
or make sleepwalkers dance
in ecstasy
or abandonment
as if some god
or some other bedazzlement
were to say
'That is not what I meant
that is not what I meant to build at all
when I made that firmament
of flesh'
as if
as if sweet love were all
there was to think of
whereas those lips
were only meant to drink of
sweet *amer*
and merriment
with no provision for
what they might touch and kiss
or graze upon
or otherwise enmesh
Please, eternal woman,
do not lead me on & on
to that mad point at which
when you might say 'I love you'

I would have to say
                    'Say something kind instead'
        or simply wish
                    yes deeply wish
                            that I were dead
            and so forever after call
                        all love a plague
                        all love a dread contagion
For it is not
            O it is not—
    so long as you
                so long as you—
                            Ah, well!—
                        There is no answer in
                        my mandolin

AT KENNETH REXROTH'S

Sweet William Blake
                    in a book in Santa Barbara
            echoes
                    in the eucalyptus

★

I roll seven chopsticks together
        and in their clicking hear
the sound of last summer's cicadas

★

I look Westward
                    into the end of day
        The Last Frontier
                    still made of Water

A PHOENIX AT FIFTY

At new age fifty
turn inward on old self
and rock on my back in a torn green hammock
deep in a ruined garden
where first the sweet birds sang
behind a white wood cottage
at Montecito Santa Barbara
sunk in sea-vine succulents
under huge old eucalyptrees
wind blows white sunlight thru
A mute ruined statue of a nymph dancing
turns in sun
as if to sing 'When day is done'
It is not
A helicopter flies
out of an angle of the sun
its windmill choppers waving
thru the waving treetops
thru which the hot wind blows & blows
pure desire made of light
I float on my back in the sea of it
and gaze straight up into eye-white sky
as into eyes of one beloved whispering
         'Let
             me
                in'
Too bright
         too bright!
I close my eyes
lest sun thru such lenses
set me afire

but the blown light batters thru
lids and lashes
I burn and leave
no ashes

Yet will arise

THE MAN WHO RODE AWAY

(To D. H. Lawrence)

        Above Taos now
                I peer through the crack
    of your locked door
           Dead Lawrence
and there indeed I see
          they've got you now at last
    safely stashed away
           locked away from the light
    of your dear sun
         in the weird great dark
     of your little
        shuttered shrine
with the dark brown cover
          of your old portable
clenched like a jaw upon
         dumb keys
            teeth sans tongue
     as in a mute mask
        of a Greek megaphone

    Ah here's real proof
         the soul has its rages—
      dampered!
        in darkness!
   shrine locked—
       booby-trapped for burglars—
plumed serpent stoned
      into a gargoyle!

                Lawrence Lawrence bearded David
                                    Phoenix flamed
            out of a mine-head
                            ash to ash
                Sown in Vence
                            and resown in America
                (del Norte)
                            Where now
                    here now
                            your portable seed
                has blown away
                            Other seeds
                are growing
                            Not yours
                Lawrence
                            in the white sands
                                    proving grounds!

Lawrence now I see you come alone
from your cribbed cabin
all fenced in the backyard compound
of that big caretaker's house

You stand still a moment in the still air.

Your eyes have a Mexican look
turned South
over the arroyos
ahora y siempre

Winter is coming

You have your ticket

You have your blue denim jacket

You have your crazy Stetson

Your tin phoenix tacked to a tree
drops in a giftshop window

A mistral wind
rattles the pine needles
of your bones

AN ELEGY ON THE DEATH
OF KENNETH PATCHEN

A poet is born
A poet dies
And all that lies between
                                is us
                                and the world

And the world lies about it
    making as if it had got his message
            even though it is poetry
but most of the world wishing
    it could just forget about him
        and his awful strange prophecies

Along with all the other strange things
    he said about the world
        which were all too true
            and which made them fear him
                more than they loved him
                    though he spoke much of love
Along with all the alarms he sounded
    which turned out to be false
        if only for the moment
    all of which made them fear his tongue
        more than they loved him
Though he spoke much of love
        and never lived by 'silence exile & cunning'
            and was a loud conscientious objector to
                the deaths we daily give each other
                    though we speak much of love

37

And when such a one dies
    even the agents of Death should take note
      and shake the shit from their wings
                        in Air Force One
   But they do not
            And the shit still flies
And the poet now is disconnected
                  and won't call back
   though he spoke much of love

And still we hear him say
         'Do I not deal with angels
           when her lips I touch'
And still we hear him say
         'O my darling troubles heaven
         with her loveliness'
And still we love to hear him say
   'As we are so wonderfully done with each other
   We can walk into our separate sleep
   On floors of music where the milkwhite cloak
         of childhood lies'
And still we hear him saying
     'Therefore the constant powers do not lessen.
     Nor is the property of the spirit scattered
     on the cold hills of these events'
And still we hear him asking
     'Do the dead know what time it is?'

He is gone under
          He is scattered
                 undersea
   and knows what time
        but won't be back to tell it
He would be too proud to call back anyway
   And too full of strange laughter
         to speak to us anymore anyway

And the weight of human experience
            lies upon the world
      like the chains of the sea
                  in which he sings
And he swings in the tides of the sea
      And his ashes are washed
                  in the tides of the sea
And 'an astonished eye looks out of the air'
                  to see the poet singing there

And dusk falls down a coast somewhere

      where a white horse without a rider
            turns its head
                  to the sea

*First read at the City Lights Poets Theatre Kenneth Patchen
Memorial Reading, February 3, 1972, San Francisco*

POEM FOR OLD WALT

SPRING DUSK DARK SHORE
LONG ISLAND NEW YORK APRIL
SKY OVER PATCHOGUE DENSE & GREY
AS WHITMAN'S BEARD
FLIGHTS OF GREY GEESE
NESTED IN IT
OVER HULK OF HIS FAIR BODY—
'FISH-SHAPE PAUMANOK'—
HULK OF HIM HOVE-TO
OFF OLD MANNAHATTA—
POETS STILL
SWIM OFF OF IT
THEIR FAR CRIES FAILING
LIKE LOST SAILORS IN A BURNING
TURNER SHIPWRECK
RED SUN FLAMES THROUGH
ON THE VERY SHORES OF LIGHT!

Poems in Transit

INTO DARKNESS, IN GRANADA

O if I were not so unhappy
I could write great poetry!
Dusk falls through the olive trees
Federico García Lorca
leaps about among them
dodging the dark as it falls upon him
O if only I could leap like him
and make great songs
Instead I swing about wildly
as in a children's
jungle gym
in a vacant lot by Ben Shahn
jump up suddenly
upon the back of a running horse
in the face of a plains' twister
And paddle away slowly
into total darkness
in a Dove boat

A GIACOMETTI SUMMER

Walking thru the Giacometti exhibition
                                        love's bodies lost
                London, summer, 'sixty-five
where are they going
                        those strange standing figures
metal shadows of themselves
                                tall as stone trees
    and too thin to have hearts

And where then am i going
                            with my fat meat
I do not have such huge feet
                            for pedestals
to keep me from falling over
                            unbalanced

Cave-light slants down on me
                                thru the bone sky
Black shadows bend those bodies
                                where love hangs heavy

Stone face gawks down on me
                                inchoately!

AN IMAGINARY HAPPENING, LONDON

In the lower left-hand corner
of an album landscape
I am walking thru a dark park
with a noted nymphomaniac
trying to discover
for what she is noted

We are talking as we walk
of various villainies
of church & state
and of the tyrannies
of love & hate

The moon makes hairless nudes

An alabaster girl upon her back
becomes a body made of soap
beneath a wet gypsy

Suddenly we rush
thru a bent gate
into the hot grass

One more tree
falls in the forest

LONDON, RAINY DAY

Nothing ever happens
            on rainy mornings like this

Life lopes on down here

Life's eternal situations
                        stutter on

Nothing changes nothing sings
Nothing takes wing

Nothing moves in the leaded air

No shadows move
                anywhere
        because there is no shade
        where there is no sun

Even the trees do not move
        even the trees do not turn
            and drop their leaves like wings

The blue rider does not appear

THOUGHTS TO A CONCERTO
OF TELEMANN

'The curious upward stumbling motion
of the oboe d'amore'
must be love itself among the strands
of emotion. It is as if its motion
were not its own at all,
as if these hands
had never struck those strings
we sing to,
swing to
(as puppets do, unbroken)
as if we never really meant to
be so strung to
those sweet pitches
love so frets us to
so tautly
so mutely
(love's bodies laid like harps!)
and then as if
there never were still more
unspoken,
as if dumb mind did never grieve
among the woodwinds,
as if its chords
did never quiver anymore
as in a buried mandolin,
as if that love
were hardly in it
anymore,
nor sounded in it

anymore,
nor heart hear it
nor life bear it
anymore.
Yet it does, it does!

CRO-MAGNONS

Cro-Magnons carried stones for books
And a flat dark stone I came upon
was one in which I read
the carbon copy histories
of creepy man
in the fine print of fossils pressed
between the stone's aged pages
the first syllables of recorded time
made into burning messages
about the first decline and fall
and the dissent of species

so that
when I cracked it open I surprised
the shadow of a lizard on the steps
of an Alexandrian branch library
burning on the broken stone
in a bright daze of sunlight
And in a flicker of that lizard's loose tongue
in one cooled instant of carbonized time
deciphered eternity

SEVERAL SURREALIST LITANIES
FOR A FILM ON THE CEMETERY
OF PÈRE LACHAISE

Ah ah
the dead
Stoned into light
Struck
in glib Te Deums
Rigid virgins
lushed at last
Angry roosts & moults
Vaults of Nothingness!
in hook of time
in ora pro nobis
Dawn's bees turn black
spider stitch
stone tattoo
in brainpan plumbing
lipread in toto
by Seine side faraway
sin side
in night light
in whiteness
laughing
liebfraumilch unbottled
trees dip their creepers hanging
underwater wound
One by one
Where— are— we— going?
groped by gay peckers
in cornhold extremis
Do the dead know

which way they're falling
falling
into lightness
in glove compartments of the moon
green grows our underwear
in diaper dung profundis
The nailed foot falls
the grass lilts wilting
the sylph skin
shuffles off
its glass bottom
bateau mouche
O drunk bateau
brak brak brak
your cold grey stones
that swinging hang below
nested underleg
salt crotch
brackish breakage by the waters of—
blithering sins and daughters of—
in catcall domini
fair frieze of scenery
Gypsy picnickers
Sunday fishers
(What mad pursuit?)
Fair fellow met
Laughing fellow rover
Rose-hip
Blear Moses
Clay somnambule!
O bread-breasted woman
kiss kiss in stone boudoirs
Saboteurs of ourselves!
How have I not seen those dead before
one by one

two by two
Have not seen them
Have been but a muted eye
on them
But I
the Eye must speak
of them
do more than see them all
Beat battlements
engraved!
trees turned to ashfoot bodies
sackbuts sewn in clothing
stashed away in white sidings
in gaudeamus igitur
cricket & violin
old Stradivarius consommé
in Père Lachaise's lap
oh the flies falter eating Love
Finger me not
I'm loose in the vulva
oh we devour ourselves!
See, see, the dead collide alive
the white void sings
leaves turn to toast
the gold ground utters
its autumn
Such seasons, such chateaux!
O sun, white tear
old rockingchair necropolis
hurls us out
through the rock cities
Night Night
rocks us rootless
(Flights of foster souls fly over)
knocks us

rocks us yes
and fingers us
(ah ah tarantula)
The earth is god's greengrocer yes
green daddy dada flocks us footloose
to the Farallones alone
and Night pours out on us
in three rivers
Myself wigged out
in photo clothing. . . .

TOC TOC: A COUPLE OBSERVED

(After Apollinaire)

Without closing its wings
                            the plane lands
            its shadow in mourning
                        for itself
            come down to itself on earth
Toc toc the clock in the tower continues
            to cast its shadow
                        onto the airfield
Toc toc another stroke of the feather
            strikes another line
                        in my face
            My shadow in mourning
                        for my self
                        tied to my feet
                        falls out of the plane
                        head first
                        ahead of my fate
Toc toc the shadows in the gardens of Père Lachaise
            draw over Apollinaire's tombeau
Toc toc the flowers of the garden are faded
            loose leaves & aeroplanes blow away
Toc toc another stroke of the feather
                        another line in a face
            a woman withdraws a man goes off
                        with his shadow
                        withdrawn into himself
                        Toc toc
                        they both turn
                        too late! too late!

TROIS POÈMES SPONTANÉS
SUR LA FORCE DE FRAPPE DE L'AMOUR
À SIX HEURES DU MATIN

I.

Bald musique chauve sourire notre dame of the night streets
dans le trentequarantième de mon âge Quatorze Juillet Caille-
botte Paris toits comme poissons glistening wet and grey sous
la pluie scales into shingles leaves into fishes fuck in the wet
beach of sky poissons se baisant sur les plages-nuages ô notre
seigneur when I rentréd in the dark dawn Cinq Rue Noire
force de frappe sous la fenêtre plus tard où passe la grande
parade de Bastille Day drap noir sinistre illusion Turn Left
phoque-phare strange tank black knight in fishscale armour
drapeau noir strange night en train de se faire en poisson armé
vive-vipère rodant sur les boulevards frappe noire ô elle avait
des grands tétons undone ô somnambule which was myself
imaginaire sweet fille her nerveuse ecstasy joyeuse force flipped
out coming and coming in the deep dawn long ago in the same
street mer glauque gown sur le tapis oh my darling pense pas
love only for we are the baiseurs not the murderers heads
blown bobbing over the sea body lost

in the crowd

II.

Endroits emerveillés nuits partagées rêveries du Night Lunch solitaire croque-monsieur tortues renversées sous tous les ponts têtes de tant-pis pieds de cochons bottés sapeurs-pompiers en train de danser triste valse des plombiers craque-monsieur Love Your Enemy même La Rousse old Dandelion Head sème à tout vent pas d'excuse autrement si tu m'amais tu faisais pas comme ça et sous tous ces ponts de tous ces Mirabeaux coule la vie et il y a trop de ponts sous lesquels la vie coule ô Inverness ô Monstre de Loch Ness sur toutes les places de la Bastille tournant et tournant dans la nuit-pas-partagée me sent vachement seul affreuse tendance de me baiser contre les vitrines but it's all right Ma dis pas que je vive in a glass house d'Alphaville où on joue perdant les bateaux mouches font pipi et on danse toujours avec son petit ami six heures du matin yeux fermés Place Contrescarpe cuisses de couscous

allez

bouffer ensemble

III.

Ceremonial de la vida nuit cassée comme un oeuf in a black
bowl the yolk-soleil se lève encore ces croque-notes casqués
marchent toujours in the light of it Squads Right le monde
takes a turn for the worse Remember the Maine chambered
nautilus couldn't turn once it started in any direction et j'suis
venu de Spain cet hiver les cloches sonnent toujours et on sait
pour qui mais on n'entend plus on danse toujours to dead
drums au Café Tambour Place Bastille le bald garçon batte son
oeuf sur le comptoir de sa vie casse-croûte the drum-world turns
après la pluie plaqué des miroirs brisés où on voit rien que les
pieds nus des célébrants figés en éternité figures faces fixed in
the dawn stagger onward titubant strung out egg-yolk in the
sky et le monde rentre dans l'obscurité du soleil jeu perdant
ballon tournant au ciel disparu au-dessus des toits fumés mais
l'éclipse des cons va arriver quand même

POUND AT SPOLETO

I walked into a loge in the Teatro Melisso, the lovely Renaissance salle where the poetry readings and the chamber concerts were held every day of the Spoleto Festival, and suddenly saw Ezra Pound for the first time, still as a mandarin statue in a box in a balcony at the back of the theatre, one tier up from the stalls. It was a shock, seeing only a striking old man in a curious pose, thin and long haired, aquiline at 80, head tilted strangely to one side, lost in permanent abstraction. . . . After three younger poets on stage, he was scheduled to read from his box, and there he sat with an old friend (who held his papers) waiting. He regarded the knuckles of his hands, moving them a very little, expressionless. Only once, when everyone else in the full theatre applauded someone on stage, did he rouse himself to clap, without looking up, as if stimulated by sound in a void. . . . After almost an hour, his turn came. Or after a life. . . . Everyone in the hall rose, turned and looked back and up at Pound in his booth, applauding. The applause was prolonged and Pound tried to rise from his armchair. A microphone was partly in the way. He grasped the arms of the chair with his boney hands and tried to rise. He could not and he tried again and could not. His old friend did not try to help him. Finally she put a poem in his hand, and after at least a minute his voice came out. First the jaw moved and then the voice came out, inaudible. A young Italian pulled the mike up very close to his face and held it there and the voice came over, frail but stubborn, higher than I had expected, a thin, soft monotone. The hall had gone silent at a stroke. The voice knocked me down, so soft, so thin, so frail, so stubborn still. I put my head on my arms on the velvet sill of the box. I was surprised to see a single tear drop on my knee. The thin, indomitable voice went on. I went blind from the box, through the back door of it, into the empty corridor of the theatre where they still sat

turned to him, went down and out, into the sunlight, weep-
ing. . . .

      Up above the town
                     by the ancient aqueduct
     the chestnut trees
                   were still in bloom
       Mute birds
            flew in the valley
                      far below
        The sun shone
                on the chestnut trees
     and the leaves
             turned in the sun
       and turned and turned and turned
         And would continue turning
   His voice
         went on
           and on
               through the leaves. . . .

WOODEN RUSSIA STILL

Knock knock on wooden Russia!
I am a white bird drilling holes
in the white wood of your snow.
To the white birches
that stretch across Siberia
from Vladivostok to Blok
I give one more knock.
Who will answer this time?
Are you still there, poet,
Are you still there, brother, anarchist,
Are you still there, under the plow?
These are not Chekhov's cherished cherry trees
that fell down long ago.
This is the eternal *taiga* now
that still stands up against all winds
dark scars upon the bark.

Knock! Knock!

Let the railsplitter
truly awake.

PERPETUAL REVOLUTION

Woke to the sound
of axes in the wood
It could have been
a hundred years ago
Chop! Chop!
Down go the Cherry Trees
And still it means
the end of an era
All comes down
And a good thing too
Let the chips fly
and down it comes
            the twisted old order
   crash
      into the underbrush

A house-cat
      gets hit by it
     but walks away from it
They
   are the great quietists
       the arch reactionaries
  the sphinxes
      that outlive revolutions
It
 shakes itself all over
      And purrs out its olive blood
      in the shape of a watch
     without hands

POEMS FROM
'RUSSIAN WINTER JOURNAL'

1.

In Khabarovsk above the Amur River, a great deserted merry-
goround park with empty Ferris wheels, airplane-ride whirli-
gigs with little planes with empty cockpits on ends of long
booms attached to a central turntable (empty planes stalled
high in air), abandoned pavilions & summer esplanades high
over the beach and frozen estuary waters, the beach covered
with snow, heroic statue of some hero in a greatcoat & boots
striding forward with a great hound wolfdog leading him but
all fenced in a little snow-covered plot among winter trees full
of stiff brown leaves frozen as blown back from the river, great
stark winter trees with sharp shadows all through the slope of
the Park frozen against bright blue winter sky, frozen park
paths through the snow under the trees, and the empty merry-
goround with one Red horse missing, and eight heroic busts
larger than life in yellow-white stone or plaster stretched along
a curved walk with green wooden-slatted benches, snow on
stone beards and eyebrows & eyes staring blind over the water,
black boats deserted drawn up on the frozen beach below, and
factories away in the distance across the water with long thin
chimneys smoking, and an abandoned outdoor dance pavilion
with small empty stage, and a very-much-larger-than-life eques-
trian statue of a mariner striding with telescope in hand above
and beyond the eight heroic busts, he too looking seaward, and
a small black & white mongrel dog who runs barking at us
from a babushka with knotted arteries, and an old old old tall
man in greatcoat & fur hat with a thousand wrinkles, and a
wood footbridge over a frozen gulley without a stream, and a
small round wooden bird-cage-house with wickets ajar through
which birds of summer long since flew to return only when the

62

cuckoo cries in the ginko tree at the top of the Park by the great iron gates through which now passes one big wolf shepherd dog embodying Rama Krishna, leading one white-bearded Walt Whitman Khabarovsk anarchist clochard with homemade bomb in pocket, as we pass out through wrought-iron gates facing the great plaza with its pinnacle stone monument to the Soviet Dead and its 100-foot-long six-foot-high white canvas banner in Russian proclaiming 50TH ANNIVERSARY OF THE GREAT OCTOBER REVOLUTION!

And uptown in front of a big café, one young father in grey lamb wool shako & fur-collared coat hurrying along the wide boulevard sidewalk under the municipal trees, carrying one wooden merrygoround horse under his arm upsidedown. . . .

2.

Recipe for Happiness in Khabarovsk or Anyplace:

One grand boulevard with trees
with one grand café in sun
with strong black coffee in very small cups

One not necessarily very beautiful
man or woman who loves you

One fine day

3.

From Baltic to the Sea of Japan the land uniting Orient & Europe is covered with huge frozen white butterflies—*schmetterlings* wing-to-wing over the plains & tundra, piled up like snowdrifts in the mountain, fluttered under birches of eternal *taiga*, falling through high passes, these frozen white butterflies like the Great White Night itself, pressing down from Arctic everywhere, Mongol humans raising round heads out of it & holding up small faded railroad flags at forlorn way stations. . . . A Red Flag is added seventeen years after the beginning of our century. . . . Sound of Mongols fucking under white birches. . . .

In this White Night Country the wood houses may someday be turned over by enormous Birds, as beasts sigh, rutting, and a Red winter sun pours blood out of Manchuria. . . .

4. THE OLD REVOLUTION

When the harvest fails in Russia
I am a sailor again
on the Battleship Potemkin
Only the ship is stuck
in Siberian snowfields
frozen wheatfields
the props won't thresh
And there's blood in the drink
I'm on the bridge as if I were admiral
And I'm down in the boiler room
stoking the old fires—
Nothing moves
And yet it won't sink!

MOON SHOT

The song that never ends
                        on & on
La vie en rose
                        and all that
It's a record
                        that's never broken
           Spin! Spin! Turn & turn & turn!
And we're
              going into cassettes
                        which will be still more unending
                                    and even reversible
'There is no end of it
                        the voiceless wailing'!
              Oooolala I can hardly stand it
                        Turn me over & play me again
There's a song in my head goes round & round
              like a fucking merrygoround
              the horses going up & down
                        wooden phalluses up & down
                                    over the dance floor
The race is on
                        between the war horses
           Which war will win
                        We're into the overtime period
              The brass ring flashes by
                        No one can catch it
              And Mother's in the street
                                    her brassiere backward

Let's get with it again
Let's get it together at last

Russia & America
Don't shoot down the moon!
There may still be lovers on it
            sleeping on the dark side
arms around each other
            turning into light

Vancouver, B. C.

A SPIDER

Spider in the toiletbowl
in Cholula Mexico!
Twice I spied him—
　　　　all head—
　　　　　　size of a BB-gun pellet—
and so many long legs—
　　　　　　stiff bent antennae!
Twice he was there
　　　　　　when I came to drown him
Twice he ducked down the drain
　　　　　　before the water hit him
　　　shrunk into nada
　　　　　　　　in a dark flash
　　　convulsed back
　　　　　　　into heart of darkness
　　shrunk back into
　　　　　　bowel of earth
into some stiff bone hand
　　　　　　that had let it go
　　　　　for the moment of a century
　　　to seek light, or what—
　　　　　　　　Bread & Glory!

Public & Political Poems

CONCRETE POLITICS

night night night night night night night
night night night night night night night
night night night night night night night
light light light light light light light
light light light light light light light
light light light light light light light
light light light DEATH light light light
light light light light light light light
light light light light light light light
light light light light light light light
night night night night night night night
night night night night night night night
night night night night night night night

A PARADE TIRADE

Good night ladies and good night nuns & priests & monks
who never march in peace parades Protestants shouldn't pro-
test The holy wars are over The only united crusade a fund
drive and good night holy ministers who evict peace groups
from their premises Onward christian soldiers and good night
good grey soldier and good night sweet prince Kennedy as long
as there are guns they will speak telescopically and good night
Colonel Cornpone and good night good night sad cop who
turned the hoses on a whole generation and flipped later and
good night asinine armistice day parades that nobody under
40 believes in Don't laugh You should take them seriously
Those big phony scenes which have nothing to do with us &
the way we want to live The america of the american legion
isn't ours This ain't 1919 Let them march off a cliff somewhere
with their obscene side arms & sinister slogans Call out the
horse marines & clean up the mess I didn't know they piled it
that high You won't get us to run your errands anymore But
here comes the band anyway A catch in the throat A lady
liberty on a float God save our country's flag she said and god
knows Veterans love wars Their eyes have seen the glory When
old comrades get together Like in the good old days So sweep
away the pickets and good day to you Doktor Teller chief
steppenwolf who stood on guard with warheads & strategies of
overkill Bomb now pay later So good night blind flight of black
avenging angels (bo-marks of death zeroed on infinity) and
good night great mute poets & professors who only stand and
wait and good night papa Hemingway who also finked out and
good night grandpa Ezra and good night reverend Eliot who
also fabricated & abdicated Hurry up please it's time and good
night stream of unconscious novelists & non-objecting painters
Thou shalt not kill except by complicity and good day Dylan
We shall not go gentle into their good night and good day

74

Neruda and good day Ginsberg who saw great heads "draw back weeping" from their plots and good day Fidel He doesn't want to marry your sister He just wants to socialize And good night good night sweet dreams crazy Karl Marx I too wish the state would wither away (into a world without countries & their great draggy nationalisms & their great draggy governments which aren't our idea of communities of love) so good night old old comrades The good old days are gone forever so goodbye goodbye death and good morning sun and goodbye senators and good morning heart that wakes at night & hears itself and good morning crocus voices and good morning waterbirds cawing & cawing and good morning lovers south of 14th street about to turn off the whole evil scene and turn on beautiful & great where the air is green

1962

TELEGRAM FROM SPAIN

NEWS FROM NOWHERE FALSE WAR RECORDS FOUND & LOST INHABI
TANTS CARRYING CHICKENS UNDER ARM BENT COCKS BETWEEN
LEGS STEALING SURVIVAL ORANGES IN ALHAMBRA GARDENS AMONG
INVENTORIES OF WORN-OUT POLITICAL SLOGANS SOWN IN VEGETABLE
GARDENS OF THE GUARDIA CIVIL SLUSHPUMPS GUMMED WITH BLOOD
OF ANOTHER GENERATION CRANKCASES JAMMED WITH NEST OF
FEATHERLESS BIRDS WHOSE BEATING WINGS STILL WON'T MAKE
THE WHEELS TURN BACKWARDS WITH SKELETONS OF STONE LIBERA
TORS FLOWN OFF THE TOPS OF IMITATION MONUMENTS ON GRAND
AVENIDAS DOWN WHICH RUSSIAN TRACTORS ONCE RAN INTO SUGAR
CANE FIELDS BURNING WITH ANARCHISTS AND FUCK YOU CRIED THE
QUEEN WHEN FERDINAND FOUND THE SULTAN IN HIS SACK AND
P.O.U.M! POUM! THE GENERALISSIMO ROSE & SANK FROM SIGHT
UNDER THE WEIGHT OF HIS OWN MEDALS MADE OF MERDE & IRONY
POLITICAL VEGETARIANS FORCED AT LAST TO FEED ON THE GREAT
PORKER HIMSELF & SO THEMSELVES DEVOURED AT LAST BY CEN
TURY PLANTS OF THEIR OWN SOWING

24 Marzo 65

WHERE IS VIETNAM?

Meanwhile back at the Ranch the then President also known
as Colonel Cornpone got out a blank Army draft and began to
fill in the spaces with men and Colonel Cornpone got down to
the bottom of the order where there is a space to indicate just
where the troops are to be sent and Colonel Cornpone got a far-
away look in his eye and reached out and started spinning a
globe of the world and his eye wandered over the spinning sur-
face of the world and after a long time he said I See No Relief
so they brought him a relief map of the world and he looked at
it a long time and said Thank You Gentlemen I see it all very
clearly now yes indeed everything stands out very clearly now
and I can see the oceans themselves rolling back and Western
Civilization still marching Westward around the world and the
New Frontier now truly knows no boundaries and those there
Vietnamese don't stand a Chinaman's chance in Hell but still
there's all these Chinamen who think they do and also think
they can actually reverse the Westward march of civilization
and actually reverse the natural Westward spin of our globe
but Gentlemen these are not War Games this is not Space
Angels this is the real thing Gentlemen and I know right ex-
actly where this here Vietnam is Gentlemen and I want to make
doubly sure that all our own people know right exactly where
this here Vietnam is Gentlemen in case any of you should hap-
pen to get cornered by some eggheads or someone And just then
Ladybird came running and Colonel Cornpone stepped into
the cloakroom and whispered to her The world really does
rotate Westward don't it? and she being smarter than he as is
usually the case whispered back that this here Vietnam was not
a place but a state of mind and Colonel Cornpone got that old
faraway look again and stepped back onto the front porch and
sat there rocking for a long time and then said Gentlemen I am
a family man and this is for real and I am hereby ordering the

complete and final liberation of Vietmind I mean Vietnam for the roots of the trouble are found wherever the landless and oppressed the poor and despised stand before the gates of opportunity and are not allowed across the Frontier into the Great Society which seems to lie out before me like a land of dreams and so Gentlemen here we go fasten your seatbelts we are powerful and free and united there ain't much we can't do and so Gentlemen let me point out to you exactly where it is we all are going on this here globe because Gentlemen even though I am reputed never to have been out of the United States I do know right where we are going on the brink of Vietmind I mean Vietnam and even though we don't want to stop the world spinning in the right direction even for an instant I do want to slow it down just long enough for me to put my finger for you right on this here sore spot which is Vietmine I mean Vietnam and Colonel Cornpone put out his hand to slow down the world just a bit but this world would not be slowed down a bit this world would not stop spinning at all and Texas and Vietnam spun on together faster and faster slipping away under Colonel Cornpone's hand because the surface of this world had suddenly become very very slippery with a strange kind of red liquid that ran on it across all the obscene boundaries and this world went on spinning faster and faster in the same so predestined direction and kept on spinning and spinning and spinning and spinning!

1966

SALUTE

To every animal who eats or shoots his own kind
And every hunter with rifles mounted in pickup trucks
And every private marksman or minuteman
                                with telescopic sight
And every redneck in boots with dogs
                                & sawed-off shotguns
And every Peace Officer with dogs
                                trained to track & kill
And every plainclothesman or undercover agent
                        with shoulderholster full of death
And every servant of the people gunning down people
                        or shooting-to-kill fleeing felons
And every Guardia Civil in any country guarding civilians
                        with handcuffs & carbines
And every border guard at no matter what Check Point Charley
                on no matter which side of which Berlin Wall
                        Bamboo or Tortilla curtain
And every elite statetrooper highwaypatrolman in custom-
                tailored ridingpants & plastic crash helmet
                & shoestring necktie & sixshooter in silver-
                studded holster
And every prowlcar with riotguns & sirens and every riot-tank
                with mace & teargas
And every crackpilot with rockets & napalm underwing
And every skypilot blessing bombers at takeoff
And any State Department of any superstate selling guns
                to both sides
And every Nationalist of no matter what Nation in no matter
                what world Black Brown or White
                        who kills for his Nation

And every prophet or poet with gun or shiv and any enforcer
            of spiritual enlightenment with force and any
            enforcer of the power of any state with Power
And to any and all who kill & kill & kill & kill for Peace
I raise my middle finger
in the only proper salute

Santa Rita Prison, 1968

80

THE THIRD WORLD

This loud morning
      sensed a small cry in
      the news
          paper
      caught somewhere on
      an inner page
          I
      decide to travel for lunch &
      end up in an automat
          White House Cafeteria
   looking thru a little window
   put a nickle in the slot
   and out comes
          fried rice
Taking a tour
      of the rest of that building
   I hear a small cry
      beyond the rice paddies
          between floors where
          the escalator sticks
  and remember last night's dream of
  attending my own funeral
   at a drive-in mortuary
    not really believing
      I was that dead
Someone throwing rice
      All the windows dry
Tipped the coffin open & laughed
          into it
    and out falls
       old funnyface
      myself

81

                    the bargain tragedian
            with a small cry
      followed by sound of Che Guevara singing
            in the voice of Fidel

      Far over the Perfume River
                              the clouds pass
                  carrying small cries
      The monsoon has set in
                        the windows weep

            I
            back up to
                        the Pentagon
            on a flatbed truck
      and unload the small brown bodies
                  fresh from the blasted fields!

1968

82

ENIGMA OF HO CHI MINH'S FUNERAL

I am walking down the middle
of Telegraph Avenue Berkeley
in the middle of the surrealist enigma
which is Ho Chi Minh's funeral
'Revolution
comes out a thirdstory window
on a recordplayer
Whatever
colors the mind
is a raga
Red Ganges
washes over mine
as water over shallows
When the mode of the music changes
someone throws bathwater out
with a burning baby in it
The People's parade
makes a U-turn
and washes up at the door
of the Free Church
where they hang up Ho's portrait
with red&black flags on the Cross
They are passing out red&green flowers
and reading Ho Chi Minh's Prison Poems
from the pulpit
An old friend I never knew very well
comes up & kisses me
waving her new Black baby
A black tank trundles by
waving its red light
and whining electronically
Back in Genoa Street

Nadja opens the door of her womb
to a great poet
It is illuminated by a very small light bulb
neither black nor red
I stand there reading
a post-revolutionary poem by Yevtushenko
which claims truth is no longer truth
when the Revolution incidentally
sets fire to a loved one's roof
At the corner of Grant & Filbert
another Nadja named Natasha Nevsky
comes to bid me a red-eyed goodbye
on her way to a bed
in the home town of Dostoevsky
I join the parade again
in my red Volkswagen tepee
A very small party of poets joins me
The photo of Ho seems to be saying ho-ho
hollowly
Waving a small black flag
which turns red subsequently
I run over my family
accidentally

1969

LETTER TO A YOUNG POET
IN CUBA OR MAYBE SPAIN

I have just discovered the Nineteen Sixties
in all the places I passed through
and all the trips I took
at the intersection of
the rotten cheese which is Europe
and the Bardo Thodol
in the intersection of
that European darkness not our darkness
and the First-and-last Frontier
which is San Francisco
in the intersection of
Hare Krishna and Kama Sutra
el orgasmo de dios
in the intersection of Quetzalcoatl and Fidel
Shiva and Allen Ginsberg
dancing in eternity
arms around each other
in the intersection of love
and of the Great White Whale stranded
between Charles Olson Jack London and Jack Kerouac
in the intersection of revolution & evolution
between too many turn-ons
and too many far-out trips
in the intersection of
two dreams and two deliriums
Drunken Boat and Sun Ra boat
hashish y bomba de hidrogeno
reino de politico de queso con mierda
I have just discovered the Nineteen Seventies
in the intersection of
the bad breath of modern poetry

and la voce del popolo
as the world sinks deeper & deeper
into the Kali Yuga
There's a high wind blowing
Watch out
when the shit hits the fan
Hummingbird Hummingbird die right on time
But the mind is still the sun
traveling through the sky
And the mind also rises
Abrazos revolucionarios
mis hermanos del Sur

1970

A WORLD AWASH
WITH FASCISM AND FEAR

This land is awash with fascism & fear
And the jails cry for freedom
Let us not deal with the obvious
                    exemplars & assholes of fascism
We will not name them with new free publicity
We all know where certain
                    fat cats are at
    Their medals
                    give them away
We all know where the Party with the capital P
                                        is at
We all know where the People with a capital P
                                        are at
They are in the country and know where
                                    it's at
And the country is rotten with fascism
as the world cries for freedom
There is too much of it
  and not enough of it
    and still we cry for it
      still they cry for it
        and eagles cry
                    America First & Last!
                    My Country, Tears of Thee!
                    And Power to the People!
                with fists raised fatally
                            as in fascist brigades
                    of the Spanish Civil War
Yes yes the world turns & turns on its fascist axis

And all the old assholes decorated with ribbons
    still sit on the top of the pile
        on top of the heaps of bods and bodies
            who cry to be drawn by Heinrich Kley
            who cry to be drawn by Goya
                who cry to be painted by Daumier
                    who cry to be smelted by Rodin-on-fire
    the old assholes with their baboon bottoms
        still blowing out the same old snorts of
                        Law & order!
                    Love Thy Neighbor or Else!
And the animal world cries for freedom
    And the Third World cries for freedom
                            and turns itself into a Fourth
                    and burns itself
And the Basques cry for freedom
And the Jews cry for freedom
Husbands cry for freedom
    And Women cry for freedom
        And illuminated Heads cry for freedom
            And faggots burn for freedom
                And men are everywhere shut up
And the world rolls on lousy with fascism
    The jails groan with it
        and governments groan with it
And wherever there's a flag with red in it
the people holding it up
                        groan with it
                    and every flag has red in it
And when they wave it
                    it drips blood
                    upon them
        The blood falls upon those
                from whom it is bled
                    from whom it is wrung

The blood falls upon those
          about whom the song is sung
And the world mops it up
  And the world rolls on with its
                    barrels of blood
For this land is our land and is rotten with fascism
  of the Left and the Right
       not to mention the unsilent Center
       not to mention the unsilent subcultures
            of uniformed guards
                 & highwaypatrolmen
                 & aerospace executives
                 & the short-haired hyenas
                      of American big business
       not to mention the unsilent undergrounds
            of speed & smack & cocaine
       and Charles Manson & Hell's Angels into junk
                 ripping off the world
  And there are no ends but means
                 I weep for you William Fritsch
And this land runneth over with fascism
                      underground & overground
     not to mention Scientology
            and its psychic authoritarianism
     not to mention one branch of the followers of
          Gurdjieff the Baron Munchausen of the mystics
       and his psychic authoritarianism
     not to mention certain aspects of Synanon
            whose Leader must have once read
       Hermann Hesse's *Bead Game* and seized upon it
          as the perfect model for a self-contained élite
            society within a society
       with its own hierarchy its own peer groups
       and its own compleat morality
            not dependent on the Outside World

Not to mention certain psychedelic
marathon encounter groupies
and their psychic authoritarianism
in the Inside World
Not to mention the Inside-out world
of great non-fascist governments
which can't exist without supporting
fascist paradises around the world
Let us not go into that
We all know about the Biggest Brothers
Their names are mouthed every night
in the jails of Turkey in the jails of Spain
in the jails of Burgos in the madhouses of nowhere
in the Women's Houses of Detention
in the jails of Vincennes
in the jails of Moscow and Marin
in the jails of Jakarta and the jails
of Germany East & West
I cannot list all the jails of the world
the jails of Greece
and the jails of Formosa
and the jails of Czechoslovakia & Poland
yes yes and the jails all the jails of this good old
land of the free
where even unions are rank with the file of force
where even the Boy Scouts of America
not to mention the American Legion
is infiltrated with authoritarian fat-asses
used-car salesmen by day
national commanders by night
in overseas caps
afraid
of Expanded Consciousness

where even the radical Left is split
      by Black Cleavers
    suppressing individual freedom
     for revolutionary ends
   And there are no Ends
               There are only means
            even when the awful means
            are awfully justified
         I weep for you George Jackson
       not to mention this country of ours by the sea
Where National Educational Television
        quakes at the slightest Congressional grumble
      and covers the cutting-room floor
       with the celluloid blood of poet-heads
    for quote artistic reasons unquote
  but the clip that falls to the floor
        happens to have the footage
          of the poet raising his Middle Finger
        to the President-General
          And who the fuck is the artist?
       I have only one life to live
       And Whistler's Mother is rocking
For this land is running with fascism & fear
  while the jails cry freedom
           Men are still chained to rock
             And Sisyphus cries for help again
         as the Rock rolls back again
         upon him
  as Quentin cries for freedom
   as Soledad cries for freedom
    and felons cry for freedom
      and offer themselves as exchanges
      for American prisoners in North Vietnam
       who are also felons
       and should not be ransomed

for they are the innocent or semi-innocent
or not-so-innocent agents of
rampant national fascisms
with which the world is so sick

as it still cries out

and still cries out

for freedom freedom

freedom

1971

BASEBALL CANTO

Watching baseball
sitting in the sun
eating popcorn
reading Ezra Pound

and wishing Juan Marichal
would hit a hole right through
the Anglo-Saxon tradition
in the First Canto
and demolish the barbarian invaders

When the San Francisco Giants take the field
and everybody stands up to the National Anthem
with some Irish tenor's voice
piped over the loudspeakers
with all the players struck dead in their places
and the white umpires like Irish cops
in their black suits and little black caps
pressed over their hearts
standing straight and still
like at some funeral of a blarney bartender
and all facing East
as if expecting some Great White Hope
or the Founding Fathers
to appear on the horizon
like 1066 or 1776 or all that

But Willie Mays appears instead
in the bottom of the first
and a roar goes up
            as he clouts the first one into the sun
                  and takes off
                        like a footrunner from Thebes

The ball is lost in the sun
        and maidens wail after him
            but he keeps running
                    through the Anglo-Saxon epic

And Tito Fuentes comes up
        looking like a bullfighter
        in his tight pants and small pointed shoes

And the rightfield bleachers go mad
            with chicanos & blacks & Brooklyn beerdrinkers
                "Sweet Tito! Sock it to heem, Sweet Tito!"
And Sweet Tito puts his foot in the bucket
            and smacks one that don't come back at all
            and flees around the bases
        like he's escaping from the United Fruit Company
            as the gringo dollar beats out the Pound
                and Sweet Tito beats it out
                like he's beating out usury
                not to mention fascism and anti-semitism

And Juan Marichal comes up
    and the chicano bleachers go loco again
        as Juan belts the first fast ball
            out of sight
                    and rounds first and keeps going
        and rounds second and rounds third
                        and keeps going
                        and hits pay-dirt
            to the roars of the grungy populace
As some nut presses the backstage panic button
for the tape-recorded National Anthem again
to save the situation

but it don't stop nobody this time
in their revolution round the loaded white bases
in this last of the great Anglo-Saxon epics
in the *Territorio Libre* of baseball

'The thought of what America would be like'
if the *Cantos* had a wider circulation
'troubles my sleep'

1971

LAS VEGAS TILT

I.

Past the highway sign that reads
                THE FATE OF THE WORLD
                    DEPENDS UPON
                THE WAY WE LIVE:
                SEE SOUTH SAN FRANCISCO
We're into the Big Sky
the whole earth catalog spread below
Day moon flies by
                    like a coin
                flipped into Vegas
Banks of cloud
                whir thru slots
                            of jetstream
        Ding-ding jackpots
                            flush up
                into blue air
Pilots up front
                with Southren accents
            in hidden cab
            pulling slotted levers
A tailwind helps us
                thru a backward hour
            with vodka on the rock
Down down so soon
                    into Vegas
with fear & loathing
                    we drop ding-a-ling
                into it
Help Help

'We are beginning our gradual descent'
down Dante's fire escape
past friendly Bogey at five o'clock
Strike
        the dingbat zone
Tumblers spin
Landscape lights up
And the world registers TILT
We dip down
thru bumpy airpockets
banks of cloud-pinballs
Buffalo Heads
in silverdollar windtunnels
five-and-dime intestines
Touch down
jiggle down on rubber wheels
dolly up to it
in life's slick chariot
of the sun
Judas Iscariot
on the run

II.

Spacecraft Earth spins on
And in the airport
the first slots light up
flashing on & off
                COIN ACCEPTED
    whir whir whir
                INSERT COIN
Indian Head rejects
                    fall out the Coin Return
where one-armed masturbators wait

Flushed out
                we stagger into it
Landed in desert
                    we find no desert
no Nile to float down
                    with Voznesensky
but Cleopatra's Barge near Nero's Nook
    with real plastic fish in its pool
            plastic raft to float on
            down Mississippis
    A Moscow poet and an American on it

Where Tom Sawyer?
                Who Huck Finn?
                        Where Injun Jim?

Jesus in dark glasses
on the bus to the Strip
carrying thirty pieces of silver
in a paper bag
In front of him an epileptic
in a gold golf cap
shaking his head continuously
uncontrollably
The silverhaired busdriver starts up
humming a tune from *Naughty Marietta*
We hum past
                Tropicana Avenue   Lone Palm Motel
        Shell Mobil   Private Pool Suites   Looney Tunes
        HEAVEN   Funny Farm   Rent-a-Car   Solarcaine
            Paradise Road Blue Chip Stamps   GOLF
        Ice   Le Cafe   THE END   Drugs   HACIENDA
        Mormon Temple   Towaway Zone   Coppertone
            Gulf   Silver Slipper   Auto Refrigeration
        Progressive Jackpots   Nevada Visitors Bureau

98

Penny Slots & Free Drinks   Las Vegas Boulevard
Play Nickels Win New Car   Hughes Air West
Bonanza Casino   Check Cashing Service
FOLIES BERGERE   "Never Before"   Sage & Sand
Hunt Breakfast   HOOVER DAM
'Old-Fashioned Hospitality'
Frontier Hotel
LAS VEGAS HILTON
THE DUNES
STARDUST
Westward Ho
SHOWBOAT
FLAMINGO
DESERT INN
PYRAMIDS
CAESAR'S PALACE
Orange Julius
Our Marriage Chapel
Little Church of the West
'Thirty Dollar Weddings'
'Go Home Satisfied or Refund'

Jesus Christ Superstar gets off

'Everyman, I'll go with thee
and be thy guide
In thy most need to go
by thy side'

III.

The end of the American dream
begins again
on the Street That Never Sleeps

And 'the extraordinary adventure of white America'
roars on
amid the proofs it never experienced the Middle Ages
A huge cowboy on a hundred-foot horse
sits astride main street downtown
raises his neon Stetson
and says electronically
       'Howdy, pardner'
His voice fills the air
      his voice is everywhere
      his picture printed in
      The Voice of the Rockies
      in the *Desert News*
      with his daily horoscope:
'Scorpions are mystery men, violent and volcanic inside, de-
ceptively cool outside. They believe in revenge and vigorous
pursuit of women. The women among them make good spies,
the men good Mafia dons or police officers, either way, and
superb athletes. Let not Aries enter these premises.'

Desert News sifts in like sand:
   CLEVELAND MAFIA RULES VEGAS
    'Geologists Say No Vegas Fault'
   'Hearst's Daughter Castigates Hearst's America
    Attacks "Absolute Spiritual Bankruptcy"'
'People change in Vegas and become what they would like
  to become and what they can't become back home'
    'Who Is Not on the Hustle
     In Life's Lottery?'
A covy of Oklahoma Mothers
with cowboy escorts
lands in The Blue Lagoon
A honeymoon couple from North Duluth
parks their blue Ford Phaeton
and struggles to the slots

100

Lady in lobby in powderblue pants & clogs
sprays her hair with a blue spray can
talking on a lobby phone
     'We come down here to a land sale.
      We dint buy no land
      but they give us free tickets
      to everything!'
A Japanese student with a skin problem
and a camera
scurries past to the john
An Indian with a skin problem
and a turban
is having trouble with his zipper
Slots whir in the Men's Room
        PRESS BUTTON TO FLUSH
And out come the coins or condoms
A minister in blue
with no skin condition
walks by jingling
a pocketful of dimes
Stands up to a slot
jiggles his pants
presses a button
and drowns

IV.

      ELECTRONIC SHOOTING GALLERY
        in the 'Circus Circus':
     'Shoot the Red Dot'
     'You're in the heart
        of the deepest and darkest
           jungles of Africa—
        Step up
             to the shooting counter, hunters—

pick up a gun, put a quarter in
                    the slot in front of you
        and take careful aim—'

'All the animals you hit
    will scream, yell, move or holler—
Take your time
            and hit all the red dots—

'Come in, hunters,
        if you're brave enough to face
            the dangers of the jungle,
        pick up a gun
            put a quarter in the slot
                    and start shooting—

'A deadly jungle killer
                    the black python
    is hanging from a tree
    waiting for someone
        to make *the wrong move*—

'Watch the animals perform—
        Pick up a gun
            and let them have it—
                You get fifteen shots—

'On your left you see a native
                with a blowgun—
        When he's aiming at you
                        shoot him—

'You're in the heart
        of the deepest and darkest
                jungles of Africa—'

KLEAN OUT KIKES
   KLEAN OUT WOPS
      KLEAN OUT REDSKINS
         KLEAN OUT SPICS
            KLEAN OUT CREEPS
               KLEAN OUT FREAKS
                  KLEAN OUT BLACK TRASH
(GEORGE JACKSON LIVES)

               'There once was a man
               who sold the Lion's skin
               while the beast still lived
               and was killed
               while hunting him'

V.

L'heure bleue
on the Strip
where time does not exist
except on the wrist of the dealer
and all that glisters is not gelt
and 'behind the tinsel is the real tinsel'
in a Monopoly Game fantasy
dreamed up maybe by some Mormon Moloch
during the Great Depression
           and stretched out there
         in the great American desert
       like some portable instant city
     set down on the face of another planet
     A five-mile long strip of gyzm
   squeezed out like dry toothpaste on a cake

In desert dust storms
     tumbleweeds
                    still blow
          across Las Vegas Boulevard
                         and still will blow
                    after a river runs thru
                    Caesar's parkinglot
               with its cargo of dead cars

The Strip lights up
                         like a pinball machine
          or a linear accelerator
                    brighter than the moon up close
          the sky a neon ceiling
                         for a room inside a lightbulb
          where it does no good to close your eyes

A helicopter from the Stardust Casino
                              moves the stars about
               over the Appian Way
     And the Roman legions come rolling
               like a Rose Bowl Parade
          with Caesar's Great Triumphal Car
               drawn by six Percherons
                         hung with elephant bells
          and leading Dürer's Rhinoceros
                                   on a string

There is a thrill in the air
The Roman legions come rolling
                         up to Caesar's Palace
Centurions
               swing off their horseless chariots
               parade up thru the gates
          come to a halt & raise their visors
                    And look about

104

The face of the pit boss stares out
chewing the butt end
of a burned-out Havana
He raises his right arm
holds it like a salute
and brings it down with a crash
There is a whirring sound
His eyes light up and spin
with dollar signs in them

VI.

Like a lost plane
with feathered wings
The Winged Victory of Samothrace
has landed somehow
in front of
CAESAR'S PALACE
built by building trades
with union funds
Martial's Palatine Sonnet
quoted in the menu
And 'Room Service a Roman Feast'
in the Frank Sinatra Suite
but no food served with Harry Belafonte
at the Midnight Supper Show
designed precisely to disgorge
the lushed-up masses
directly into the
carrousel Casino
groaning with gaming tables
Roulette Baccarat Keno
in a sea of slotmachines

                    one of which once in a while lights up
                shakes all over
                            showers out Caesar's own silverdollars
                        and emits a puff of smoke
Whiskey America plunges in
                            into the Soft Machine
            into the steaming pits
                as into a scene from Dante
                            painted by Gustav Doré
                            whose clouds were angels
            Caesar not Virgil thy guide

        Wearing blue and carrying a feather
                will not win
            Belafonte himself falls in
                and drops $27,000
                at Baccarat
            and next night sings a song-cry
                    about the pit bosses:
                    'If it moves and is warm
                    I will fleece it'
                    And all that glisters
                        is not guilt
                    at the baccarat tables
                    two dealers deal
                the final Big Brother trip
            And two pit bosses watch them
        and three foremen watch the pit bosses
        and one pit boss watches three foremen
            from behind two-way mirrors
                on the low ceiling
            under which circulate the masses
                mixed with house-dicks

                    Hoc in terra Caesar est

The pudgy pit boss squats
                    on his highchair throne
        rings on fat fingers
                    and a fat cigar clutched loose
a De Mille Caesar
                with lizard looks watching wrong moves
    Drear players with coin-eyes
                    stuck like horned toad zombies
                    round the board
    'Phlebas the Phoenician a fortnight dead'
            holds his cards and hangs his head
    Dawn breaks outside somewhere
                    and the deal continues
Gold sun bursts forth unseen somewhere
                    through a cottonwood grove
    And the big shuffle goes on
    The walls themselves fall down
                    as in Buster Keaton movies
            and they still play on
                    Pale Faces turning paler
                impaled on rotating spits in pits
                roasted with rotating oranges
                    apples & cherries
                    under glass
                through which also wink & blink
                Buffalo Heads & Indian Heads
        in hock in terror   in bas-relief
            And Eisenhower eyes and Kennedy eyes
            And the weird Third Eye that winks not
                from its Transamerica Pyramid
                    in the dollar's
                            green desert
        upon which hangs a sign
                        WE NEVER CLOSE

VII.

And now at Angels Peak in morning light
thirty miles above Vegas
Andrei Voznesensky asks no quarter
but takes a coin of his own
and drops it in the mouth of the daughter
of the President of Caesar's Palace
and pulls her right arm down
and waits for the virgin coin
to fall out below
if he's that lucky

And at Indian Rock Refuge
we get out
and climb up the steep riprap
to the Indian cave at the top
from which the flat world can be seen
and drop small round flat stones
into slots in it

And await the final
deluge jackpot landslide
of earth and life

in which the fate of the world
depends upon
the way we live

1971

FORTY ODD QUESTIONS
FOR THE GREEK REGIME
AND ONE CRY FOR FREEDOM

Can you tell me the way to the American Express?

Can you show me the way to a real Greek taverna filled with picturesque dancing descendants of the first democracy on earth?

Where do we catch the boat for Plato's Republic?

Is it true that your great Greek tragedies and tragi-comedies are now being performed daily in police stations?

Where is Katsimbalis Where Zorba Who stole Euripides?

Is it true the Victory of Samothrace turned to turds April Twenty-first?

Why did you steal the Elgin Marbles?

Have you ever looked into Chapman's Homer?

What have you done with my island?

Are you a bunch of smart guys putting us on or imbeciles who really mean it?

What have you done with the young poets in small boats and the old poets on bicycles?

How are things in the torture chambers of Bouboulina Street?

Did you know Jacqueline Onassis once was married to a democrat you would have liked to torture?

Why is there not room in Greece for the grave of one more free man?

Who moved the Trojan Horse to Athens?

Will Aphrodite ever find her arms?

Where is the light of Greece, the violet light of Attica?

Why can't we just sail away to the Isles of Greece and forget everything?

Why did the King cut out so fast, with his suitcases, his little dogs, and his great mother?

Why isn't the Constitution printed on a rope?

Have you seen Ulysses' dog lately with all his eyes on you?

Why can't I drink retsina lately without getting more thirsty?

Why hasn't the Oracle of Delphi spoken out lately?

How come more American poets don't attack you?

Why won't you just Go Away if we ignore you?

Where is the light of Greece, the violet light of Attica?

Is it true you'll screw anything that moves even on Sunday?

Why isn't your Constitution printed on money?

110

Who will rescue the phoenix from the fascist soldiers that spring out of its flames on every matchbox signpost and mailbox?

Can you still hear the cocks of Athens crow from the Acropolis?

Do you know what they're crying?

Where is the light of Greece, the violet light of Attica?

Can you still read Greek?

Does "Z-Z-Z-Z-Z-Z" mean the sound of sleep to you?

Does "Z-Z-Z-Z" make you think we're sleeping?

Does *Zoë* still mean Life in your language?

Does *Zei* still mean "He lives" in your language?

Do you think *Elefteria* means Leftover Freedom?

Have you forgotten the word for Liberty?

Can your tongue still pronounce it?

We still can still announce it

Elefteria agapi mou!

First read at a benefit for the Greek Resistance, Fugazi Hall, San Francisco, April 20, 1972

111

CARNAVAL DE MAÏZ

In the churches of Cholula
                    the bleeding Christs groan
                              their Indian misericordias
          as Christian saints in cages
                    wring their wood hands
                         over bloodblack rosaries
          wailing & bewailing
                              Great God Death
                         in Churrigeuresque chapels
                         wherein sweet Indian faces
                         had their burro-vision bent
                         into 'Heaven-sent'
                         baroque monstrosities
White Christ Quetzalcoatl was predicted
     and did indeed land
               and did indeed take that land in pawn
And still riseth up ruined & raunchy
     with barbaric yawn
               in the dawn of a new debacle
As we walk into it chewing chicle
               carrying cameras & Oaxaca blankets
And also groan aloud
                    but only for
                         what we would ignore
And still hold our breath
                    and tread with stealth
               among the wealth of what we call
                              'medieval superstition'
As we in Norteamerica now
                    have indeed abolished Death
          and no longer need
                    such monuments & consolations

We have banned it forever from our lives
                and seldom see anyone dying anymore
                        except on TV in some foreign country
        And freeze our bodies to unthaw uncancered
                a thousand years hence
        And decay and dissolution
                                have no sight of us
                who are in effect immortal
        Only the gods lie & die in us
And still *La Patria es primera*
                        all over this divided earth
        where the poor will be born without ass-holes
                if shit should ever become valuable
                And they stay stuck in the ground forever
        in that ground which is graded & regraded
                                traded and retraded
                        deeded & misdeeded
                                all over Mesoamerica
        where every revolution still
                        boils down to the scam
                of 'getting land without men
                        for men without land'
            who will still spring up
                        like teeth on ears of corn
    in the hands of that International Harvester
        whose mouth unsinging
                        ever hangeth open
                avaricious
                        and slobbering!

11 Mayo 72

ALASKA PIPE DREAM

One fine day like the day after tomorrow while the Canadian Energy Minister was minding his own business by saying the Alaska Oil Pipeline was really an 'internal matter' in the USA and not for Canadians to jump into, one fine day in the not very distant future while the Energy Minister was talking he suddenly noticed that one leg of his trousers was wet, and hoping it was not what he thought it was, having for some time been housebroken, he reached down and determined that in fact it was not an internal matter at all but an external matter of oil, and yet not pure oil for when he inspected his hand he found it not only oily but bloody, and when he rushed to the lab to find out why blood was mixed with oil and whether or not it was *his* blood mixed with *their* oil or *their* blood mixed with *his* oil or whatever, he was informed by the lab hired by the oil company that there was really nothing to worry about at all, since the blood would not stop the oil from working perfectly in American war machines and automobiles, not to mention the Mayor of Montreal's Ford, and in any case the blood was not the Canadian ministry's blood and it was not the American people's blood, it was simply the blood of one billion waterfowl who had been unable to feed in the tundra which had been disrupted by the perfectly innocent Pipeline, and it was simply the blood of one billion fish in Canadian waterways and one billion fish in Canadian seaways who were no longer able to eat the plankton now flavoured with salted oil, and it was simply the blood of one billion deer in the Northern Territory and one billion other wild animals in other frozen territories in the Siberia of Canada which had gradually become unfrozen for the first time in recorded time due to the world's largest Oil Spill which had resulted from earthquake Pipeline rupturings which caused a great wash of hot underground oil to pour Eastward from

Alaska all over the geologic underground strataface of Canada, so that the St. Lawrence dripped both oil and animal blood into the water supply of the City of Montreal, but this was strictly an Internal American Matter, and we were not concerned at all, at all. . . .

Montreal, March 1973

American Mantra & Songs

Interested in developing chants with American English words as opposed to singing Sanskrit or other unknown tongues, I at one time or another sang spoke or chanted these verses in varying versions, sometimes with much spontaneous repetition not herein noted, often with autoharp accompaniment.

MOTHER OF LIGHT MANTRA

Father of love

        Mother of rain

Father of night

        Mother of pain

Father of day

        Mother of light

Mother of phantoms

        Mother of phantoms

Dark ages over now

Dark ages over now

Dark old daddy

Father of phantoms

Mother of light

Dark ages over now

Dark old daddy

Rainman dance and sing!

(*After Zimmerman*)

BIG SUR SUN SUTRA

Sun Sun

Ah sun Om sun

Sun Sun Sun

Great God Sun

Still riseth in our Rubaiyat

and strikes and strikes

And strikes the towers

with a shaft of light!

Strikes us in our Sun-ra boat

Strikes and strikes us in our Sun-ra boat

Sun Light Life Light

Sun Sun Sun

Great God Sun!

LAUGHING & CRYING

I laugh to hear me say what I am saying

Walking in my cave of flesh

There must be a place

There must be a place

Where all is light

I laugh to hear me say what I am saying

O Rama

Audiart O Audiart

dancing Shiva dear one

Your face flies through the sky

I laugh to say what I am saying

Each of us a lamp

a spirit-lamp

a lantern burning

a lamp a place beyond a turning

where all is light

I laugh and cry

with mask of tears

and laughing face

I laugh and cry to hear me say what I am saying

My laughing face

and mask of tears

makes me laugh and cry to hear me sing what I am saying

For there must be a place

There must be a place

where all is light

NIGHT LIGHT

Night, night

Death's true self, Death's second self

Black is my true love's hair

Yet all, all is despair

Black night, black light

Death's true self

Black, black, black is my true love's hair

And all, all is despair

Night, night

Death's second self

where all is empty, all is despair

All gone, all down

All, all despair

And grey is my true love's hair

Yet sun bursts forth upon the land

And a butterfly lights in it

upon my hand

And lights these songs

and lights these songs

in air

TANTRIC BALLAD

Man and woman meet and part

coupling with their counterpart

in the calyx of the lotus

And the lotus opens and opens

its very heart of light

Lovely lotus opens, opens

and then closes

into night

Man and woman meet and part

coupling with their counterpart

in the calyx of the lotus

which can only close when it opens

which can only open when it closes

Man and woman meet and part

And dear friends die

And night is where our lovers lie

And light is where our lovers lie

in the calyx of the lotus

which opens and opens

and closes and closes

when we live

and when we die

IDOL CHANT

Idol whose feet have golden rubies on them

That golden person who is seen

within the sun

with golden mouth and golden hair

Idol whose feet have golden rubies on them

whose eyes are like blue lotuses

Golden altogether

White light of sun

and blue exceeding darkness

Idol whose feet have golden rubies on them

speak O speak

'the full account of Om'

(After Upanishads, Prapathanka, Kanda 8)

GREAT CHAIN CHANT

Great chain of being Great chain turning

O cycle made of meat

O snake who eats its tail

Great chain of being Great chain turning

O snake who eats its tail

O hungry self

without an end or a beginning

Great chain of being Great chain turning

O hungry self

O wheel of meat

made of us

Great chain of Being

with no end and no beginning

All beings being one

Turn & turn & turn!

AIRPORT MANTRA

(Seeing Allen Ginsberg off to India)

Plane says Om

Sky says Om

Sun says Om Om

When will America sing it

When will America utter it

Om is He who is meat & air

Om is She who is Light

Om is universe spinning

Sound of universe singing

Love-sound of Om

Sigh-cry of Om

Mutter and moan of Om Om

Breath of life which is Om

Om America unknown

singeth in the void

SPONTANEOUS ANARCHIST
PACIFIST BUDDHIST SONG
(To be delivered in the Russian heroic style)

War! War! War!

World! World! World!

Life, Light, Love, Men & Women!

All one

One boat of meat!

Rock rock rock!

Past Present Future All time All one

All places planets things & beings one

All color sound and taste and touch

all one

All form and emptiness

All living entities All sentient beings one

Old Age Annihilation Death & Suffering

All Sensation Thought & Tears & Laughter

Ecstasy

Sweet dear words Sweet caresses too

All one

All Light All made of Light

One breathing Universe

Highest Perfect Wisdom breathing

All poems & songs

All lips & tongues & voices One

Mystic texts of our bodies

make love not war!

(After The Great Paramita Sutra)

131

NINE SHAMAN SONGS RESUNG

(Upon Last Looking into Arthur Waley's Translation of 'The Nine Songs')

I.

Strike the Dark Strings

Strike Strike

the dark strings

And reed & zither answer

Spirit moves

in splendid gear

And is the body's splendid shaman

through which a god may sing

And indeed does sing

And strikes and strikes

that Darkest Bell

ah darkest bell—

my body struck

with love

II.

Flower-spirit, shaman-child

in blaze of brightness dancing

Endless as the earth

She dances round it

As sun

As mantic moon

in dragon-chariot of sun

O ondloᴏᴏ flight!

Part of me climbs to heaven

through the four seas & seasons

Longing for you

III.

She-shaman princess

in a stone boat

in winged dragon-boat

awning of fig-vine

sweet flag paddles

magnolia rudder

Rides to that Island

to that Bright Island

abode of light

Swinging her mesmere lamp

her incense burner

on a gold chain

She drops her thumb-ring in the Sea

And turning

and turning

stretches her body burning

toward me

(though she told me told me

she was not

free)

And flying dragons sweep her far away

from me

I gallop my horse in the morning

through the lowlands by the river

IV.

I build a bride-room

                underwater

     roof thatched with lotus

          courtyard paved with murex

At dark dusk I cross

             to the Western bank

   Here it was

         she cast down

              her thin dress

              upon the shore

   Over the white nut grass

           my eyes wander

     see only water swirl

             in the flood rains

Someone says my loved one sent for me

I gallop my horses

          over the lotus leaves

    toward where a dragon waits

         toward where an elk browses

On the Mountain of Nine Doubts

V.

Lord Sun

wheels in flight

trailing his spirit-garment

High over the Nine Hills

he handles Yin & Yang

male & female

shade & sunshine

soul & body

a Yin for every Yang

And gallops into Light

I pluck the lovely hemp flower

Age creeps on apace

Soon all will be over

Soon all done all one

And fate is fixed in the heart

And not to draw nearer

      is to drift forever

             further apart

VI.

Hall full of lovely ones

Yet you had eyes for me alone

Riding a whirlwind A cloud for a banner

Suddenly you came

And as suddenly departed

And only had eyes for me

I bathed with you

in the Pool of Heaven

In a sunny fold of the hill

I dried your hair

Now it is I who shout & sing with despair

Under a chariot-awning

of peacock feathers & halcyon flags

You climb again to the Nine Heavens

VII.

A glow in the sky

        and soon you'll arise

Night pales

        Day shines forth

You ride on thunder wheels

        cloud banners trailing

    heave great sighs

        look back yearning

        for earth's beauty burning

    look and linger

        forget your way

I draw a long arrow

        and shoot Heaven's Wolf

then draw me down the Dipper

        And plunge alone into

        the White Void

VIII.

With you wandered

        down rivers and coasts

  River God

      in fish-scale boat

  drawn by dragons

        with griffin oarsmen

With you I wander

      on the river islands

  go with you as far

       as the Southern Shore

Dark dusk falling

And I too sad

    to think of returning

  Eyes only for

      that farthest shore

  I lie awake

      yearning

IX.

Mountain Spirit left me alone

             dark in a bamboo grove

Air dark with rain

              Monkeys twitter again

cry all night again

           And cry and cry

              all night again

Waiting for you

           I wander and linger

turn and turn

          and turn again—

And won't turn back

            and won't turn back—

Without my beloved

STREETS OF SAN FRANCISCO

'Streets of Paris pray for me'

Streets of San Francisco wait for me

Streets in rain and streets in pain

Streets in sin and streets in sun

Streets of Paris Streets of San Francisco

pray for

wait for me

Sun on beaches Sun on mesas

shine on me

rain on rivers

wash me away

Plain tree plain tree

shade me

River of thinking

        drown me drinking

river of drinking

        drown me thinking

rain on ocean

        wash me away

Sun on Sunday

        warm and dry me

moon on Monday

        darkly light me

lightly light me

        light my way. . . .

(After Palinarus)

BALLAD OF THE BOAT-KEEPER

(In a Brechtian mode)

Last night at midnight

Some people came along the dock

                           laughing and talking

Only one of them was saying

    'Life, life is a fucking tragedy—

    And I come to that conclusion

    as an optimist—'

'No, no,' said another, laughing.

But the first went on:

    'Life is a bloody blood-bath for sure,

    And we are all washed in it—'

'No, no!' said another, laughing.

But the first went on:

    'We sleep in blankets of blood

    And we swim in it

    And all goes down!'

'No, No!' said another, laughing,

And she sang a sweet melody.

But the first went on:

    'Yes, yes, all, all goes down,

    And you too will founder—'

'No, No,' said another, laughing,

'I'll never drown,

I'll never go down,

My life not end, in weeping—'

And his voice died away

           on the Bay

And his voice died away

           in my sleep

And his voice died away

    And his voice died away

        died away

          died away

And his voice and his self

          died away